Get Paid To Perform!

A Performer's Reference Guide to Getting Booked

By Dan Cain
Mentalist

Get Paid To Perform

(Get Paid To Perform! A Performer's Reference Guide to Getting Booked)
Copyright © 2013 by (Dan Cain)

All rights reserved. No part of this book may be reproduced or transmitted in any form or by any means without written permission from the author.

Table of Contents

Rama Setu	3
Knowing Your Craft	5
Presentation	7
Get Out!	13
Phone Script/Dining Est.	14
Phone Script/Cold Call	17
Performance Options	19
Performance Agreement	22
Speaking & Listening	25
Independ. Contr. Agreement	31

Rama Setu

Rama Setu, also known as Adam's Bridge and made of a chain of shoals, 30 km long, in the Palk Straits between India and Sri Lanka, reveals a mystery behind it. The bridge's unique curvature and composition by age reveals that it is man-made. Legend as well as Archeological studies reveal that the first signs of human inhabitants in Sri Lanka date back to the primitive age, about 1,750,000 years ago and the bridge's age is also almost equivalent. That's right, 1,750,000 years ago. According to Hindu legend, the bridge was built to transport Rama, hero of the *Ramayana,* to the island to rescue his wife from the demon king Ravana.

I want this book to be a sort of Adam's Bridge for those individuals that want to travel from where they are today to the place where they want to be in their entertainment careers.

Most of us are sitting there thinking, 'When will I start making some money doing what I love to do?' I am of the opinion that it's up to the individual to decide when. Whether the individual lacks the resources and simply needs to find them, or if the individual lacks the self-esteem to make the move toward success it still rests on them.

I will provide EVERYTHING you need to get started making money in the magic business. I may even throw in a magic routine at the end of the book. We'll see.

Many of you know the mechanics of your art. The sleights, the pulls, the switches, the fancy flourishes. But what you don't do is ask the right people to pay you for what you do. I will give you the scripts that I use, the Performance Agreements that I use and even the Contractor Agreements I use to employ others to sell for me. I think this is a first in our industry.

You will have everything you need in this book to start setting yourself up for success immediately. That means – today. So, without further adieu…

Knowing Your Craft

First things first. You must know your craft. Whatever that may be. I'm not a flourishing card kind of guy. I have no need for that in my shows or presentations. That doesn't mean I can't handle a deck of cards. I am of the same opinion as Bob Cassidy in that I shouldn't showcase my ability with cards. I am a reality engineer (*Thank you Mark Kemish aka Mr. E. Mann for that term*) and I have to give the illusion that the miracles I seemingly perform with cards are just that – miracles. If I use cards ostentatiously, then the spectators will assume I am just a card trickster that can manipulate a deck well.

Lesson:
Just because you know how to do something, doesn't mean you should reveal it openly.

Know your craft. I'm a mentalist. I should know as much as I can about what I should be able to do. I don't know everything, but I'm always learning. Every day I read something new regarding my craft, my art. You should too.

You have to remember also, chances are there are other individuals trying to do what you're doing too. So you must be better than them. If you have a full-time job and you want to make money performing then you have to work that much harder than the other guy or gal. That's just how it is. If you have a family then you have to learn how to balance your personal life with your entertainment life. It can be tough at times, but it can be done.

You should concentrate on what makes you better at your craft. Do Not –I repeat – Do not buy every new routine or effect or magic trick that surfaces to the home page of whatever magic distributor you purchase from. That will empty your pockets and your focus will not be on marketing yourself. Chances will also be that you're buying things you'll NEVER use in a performance. By a show of hands, who has a bunch of items they purchased that will never be used? I thought so. How do I know? Well, I'm a mentalist. No, seriously though, I went through that myself. I would purchase effect after effect and when I had thousands of dollars invested in things I thought were cool at the time I realized that those things will not return my investment. What happened next? Buyer's remorse in a bad way.

Notwithstanding, I decided to turn what I knew into a money generating company.

So, from this point forward:
- STOP PURCHASING ITEMS BECAUSE THEY'RE THE NEWEST EFFCT
- POLISH AND REFINE WHAT YOU KNOW ABOUT YOUR CRAFT
- BALANCE YOUR TIME
- PRACTICE PRACTICE PRACTICE.

Presentation

Presentation is a key to success. This encompasses everything from what you know about your craft to how you dress; from how you speak to what you associate yourself with.

I have an image I present to the world. That image is someone that wears a suit, minus the vest and tie. I wear sateen shirts of various solid colors always buttoned to the top. A nice belt, pair of black dress shoes and a clean haircut. I speak a certain way, walk a certain way, and gesticulate in a certain manner. I am always ready to do any number of "impromptu" routines with a limited arsenal I keep on me.

I most likely have a loop, business cards, and a pen. I can control a person's perception of reality with only those three items. I can perform a levitation, telekinesis, dual reality routines, predictions, personal revelations about a person, one ahead routines, etc!

Someone else, depending on their craft should be prepared in like manner. A legerdemain should have a deck of cards at the ready. A children's magician should have something child-friendly.

However you decide to brand yourself you have to be prepared to always be recognized in that light. If you decide to be a family magician specializing in children's parties, then you have to understand that's how you will be viewed.

I know a fellow magician that works for $90 per hour doing children parties. He's great at what he does but complains he's not making enough and can't seem to raise his costs. What he doesn't grasp, and I've tried to explain to him is that his target market is families with a small budget. Parents of children that expect to pay $50 for the day for a small magic show are cringing at the bold request for $90 per hour.

Your presentation should work hand in hand with your target market. If you want to perform at family restaurants, then dress accordingly and understand close-up illusions with one on one spectators. If you want to perform at fine dining establishments then I would suggest creating a center floor presentation and understand effects that work for small to medium audiences.

If you want your value to increase in the children's party theme then associate yourself with that market. If you want your value to increase in the corporate market then associate yourself with that market. When you align yourself with your target market, then you build value in your ability within that market.

Promotional Material

Before we discuss promo material I have to tell you if you have a phone, you have a means to conduct business. If you have a means to conduct business, you have a money generating opportunity.

I utilize the services of a company called www.vistaprint.com for printing my business cards. The quality is superb and the cost is extremely effective and within my budget. I get matte finish and printed on one side. The back of my card is blank for me to perform any given effect I choose. Also, keep in mind that less is more. On the front of my business card is an image of myself, my name, my title and my website:

Get Paid To Perform

I do not have my phone number on my card for a couple reasons. One reason is that I don't want to be too accessible. If I'm too accessible that means I'm not busy. If I'm not busy it gives the impression that I'm not in demand, thus not wanted. The other reason is that I want people to be directed to my website.

I've seen so many performers list as much as they can on the front and back of their business cards. In my honest opinion I think it's tacky and too busy. I like to lead individuals to something even better than what they're experiencing at the moment. This is a good example of that. I have a website that I pay for every month. I want people to visit my website. The more traffic my website gets, the higher the chances I'll get booked. One way to direct traffic to my website is my business card. There is no contact information on my business card. My website is printed on the bottom of the card to direct their attention to it. Once on my website the prospect will immediately see an amazing promotional video on my homepage. There are links to other videos including testimonials and performances.

Use what you have. If you have a camera, take some decent photographs of yourself. Ask someone to help you if possible. This will help you begin to build your promo package. List the types of shows you can do. Knowledge of your craft will help you here. By the time you're finished you will probably have about 9 pages worth of information to hand out to a potential client. This is not acceptable. I know this through personal

Get Paid To Perform

experience. My first promo package was about 9 pages long. I wanted to present so much at once. But as I learned, LESS IS MORE.

Eventually I cropped my info down to a tri-fold –one page- brochure as is seen here:

Outside Brochure

You're Guests Will Never Forget!

No one in the audience knows who will share the stage with him next. This allows for the audience, as a whole to experience the show on a large scale while allowing an individual to enjoy it on a more personal level. EVERYONE leaves with a feeling of awe!

Dan has combined his stage experience in the art of mentalism with his close-up illusions to bring you mind blowing entertainment. NO camera tricks! People will talk about your event long after the night is over.

Just imagine......

Contact

Mailing:
Cain Illusions, LLC
PO Box 215
Hartly, DE 19953

Office:
(302) 526.7910

Email:
dan@cainillusions.com

Website:
www.cainillusions.com

Cain Illusions, LLC

"Legend! That's the cheekiest boldest thing I've seen in mentalism for a while! A stroke of genius!"
-Christo Nicolle, Thaumaturgy, UK

Dan Cain, WWW.CAINILLUSIONS.COM

Get Paid To Perform

Inside Brochure

He is the only person who has predicted the winner, final score, & specific highlight of SuperBowl 46. He has stopped his heartbeat for 17 seconds and restarted it in front of a live audience!

"You have one of the most powerful minds and connections to the universe that I have ever experienced in my life."
Tiffani Fischer
CEO of Fischer-Reynolds, Inc.

How would you like to add something unique, entertaining & awe inspiring at your next event?

Dan Cain is a professional Mentalist & Illusionist. He has combined both art forms in an effort to present a show that will keep your guests wanting more.

From the very start, _everyone_ in the audience is involved. A guest thinks of a loved one and Dan reveals it. He creates a connection where one person is touched and another feels it.

He proves randomness is not random at all! He can even show a bit of comedic relief by turning the entire audience into Thought Readers instantly!

His show is one hour in duration and incorporates stage presentation with high impact interactive mentalism!

If you have the means to create the brochure, do it. Otherwise vistaprint.com offers very affordable options if you have internet access.

Dan Cain, WWW.CAINILLUSIONS.COM

I can discuss more about other promotional material here, but I think it's not necessary at this point. I want you to start making money asap! A business card is what I always carry with me. A brochure is not. But I have them at the ready if someone wants one mailed.

Get Out!

Who are you interacting with? How often are you interacting with them? What do you say when you explain what you do?

Are you frequenting the places you want to perform for? Are you talking with the right people that hire people like yourself?

When people would ask me what I do I would tell them flatly that I'm a Mentalist. Even today, people still struggle with the term "Mentalist." They just have no idea what that means. When I would try and explain it to them. They would have a puzzled countenance and look at me as if I had 10 heads. Then I would say things like "I'm an honest psychic." Because if a psychic were honest they would tell you they were performing mental illusions. Nowadays I respond by saying, "It's a bit difficult to explain what I do for a living. It's better if I show you." Then I'll proceed with an Acidus Novus routine. Presentation is EVERYTHING.

There are a few different ways to GET OUT.
- You can physically visit places you'd like to associate yourself with.
- Phone calls (cold-calls)
- Restaurants
- Publicity Stunts (See my book *"How I Predicted Super Bowl 46 – A marketing strategy for novices and professionals"*)

Each way has its own way of getting you out there and cost little to no money to do so. If you feel like you're not where you want to be in your career, it's probably because not many people know who you are. You need to make yourself known.

When making cold calls you have to decide who you're going to approach. If you want to perform for corporate events, you're not going to call the local Dunkin' Donuts. If you're going to target children's parties, you're not going to call Reckitt Benckiser. First decide who you're going to contact. Then decide the proper path for contacting them. I'm going to assume that the reader is interested in performing for companies (restaurants, corporations, etc).

There are many ways to collect info on companies you want to reach. Salesvantage.com will offer you a list of event and meeting planners. A simple Google search with various search parameters will give you particular information regarding those targeted companies. A paid provider I use from time to time is Salesgenie.com. They offer names of contact persons, annual revenue, loose credit score gauge, etc. Once you have your target market it's time to make some calls. Here is the script that I designed for myself. It works wonderfully. This is the script that I use. This is the script that I secure gigs that generate $850 - $1,500 **for only an hour of my time at fine-dining establishments.**

Phone Script for calling Fine Dining Establishments

Always ask for the <u>Event Coordinator</u>, <u>General Manger</u> or the <u>Owner</u> depending on the company. If they are not available leave your name, number and company name.

If you are connected to the decision maker (EC, GM or Owner) continue with the following:
Hi, this is _____ with (your company name). Do you ever have entertainment as an after dinner show?
- **If they answer "Yes"** then continue with the script below.

Get Paid To Perform

- If they answer "No" then ask: "Would you consider the option of having a "dinner & show" night?" Then continue with the script below.

Do you have a room that can be closed off from the rest of the guests and can seat 50 or more patrons? (if the answer is no then hang up the phone)

My company and I offer an interactively dynamic Mentalism show for fine dining establishments such as yours. I'm the only one in the history of the NFL and Mentalism that predicted the outcome of the Super Bowl THREE MONTHS BEFORE THE GAME. I SELL OUT SHOWS WHEREVER I PERFORM! I don't ask to be put on your payroll. As a matter of fact I want to pay <u>you</u> for allowing me to perform at your venue.

They may ask: How does it work?

It works like this. For example seating would be at 7pm and the establishment would offer a limited menu so it wouldn't be too burdensome for the kitchen. At 8pm the after dinner show would begin and last for 1 hour. A server would continue through the hour by serving dessert and drinks. The cost per person for the show would be $15. The establishment would add it into the cost for dinner. We would give the establishment $3 from each ticket sold. Thus, we would receive $12 for each person present. Payment would be due on the same night of the performance.

The advertising would be <u>extremely easy</u>. We would take care of newspaper mentions. Your front desk person would help by simply offering the dinner & show as a dining option to callers making reservations or individuals walking in. We would supply flyers that could be set up in your lobby, on counters, or in windows for easy reference.

What night do you have in mind for a dinner and show?
(if the answer is a positive one then book the event)
(if the answer is not then follow up with ->When would you like to set up a meeting?)

(if you can't secure a gig for sometime in the next 2 weeks while talking with this establishment at least try to secure a date to meet with them in person)

PERSONAL NOTES:

If I cold-call a company this is the script I use:

Hi, this is Dan Cain with Cain Illusions. I need to speak with your Head of Corporate Communications. (If they don't know who you're referring to, ask for the Event Coordinator).
(If they still don't know who you are referring to, ask – "Who is in charge of planning events?")

They will either transfer you or simply give you the name of the individual.

What's his/her phone number?

Contacting the decision-maker:

Hi, this is Dan Cain with Cain Illusions. I understand you're the person in charge of planning events for your company.
Our company provides a dynamic impact mentalism show for companies like yours.
Your event can benefit from his show in many ways.
PROSPECT: *"How can my event benefit from his show?"*

YOU: Ok, let me know what the setting of your next event will be like (Hotel Banquet Room? Hotel Bar, Office, etc?)

QUALIFYING QUESTIONS:

How many people will be there?
Who will be there (Adults? Children?)
Will there be other entertainment?
Where and when is it going to be held?
How did you hear about me? (If they were referred and called you)
Would you prefer Stage or Strolling? (I'm getting them to imagine me performing in their own mind with this question)

(Depending on the answers given can determine your response here. By getting as much information you can about the event will give you clues about the budget they have for entertainment and help you determine what you should be charging and what you will be doing)

Performance Options

- **CLOSE UP/STROLLING** --His specialty in this area is performing illusions right in front of your face and underneath your nose that will leave you in disbelief. There are no camera tricks when it comes to his form of artistry. As he strolls the room(s) the seeming miracles happen only inches away from you. **We all know the time it takes to find entertainment for an Event like yours. Scheduling this show at this time will reduce cost by eliminating the time it would normally take for you to research and find entertainment for your Event. People will come up to you and congratulate you on a great event – EVEN IF YOU DON'T WANT THEM TO! People will talk about the event YOU hosted long after the night is over.**
- **STAGE** – Dan's act is 50 – 60 minutes of mind-reading and psychological manipulation, complete with audience participation and humor. This option typically follows a dinner. No one in the audience knows who will share the stage with him next. This allows for the audience, as a whole, to experience the show on a larger scale while allowing an individual to enjoy it on a more personal level. **EVERYONE LEAVES WITH A FEELING OF AWE!** A guest thinks of a loved one and Dan reveals it. He creates a connection where one person is touched and the other feels it. This is as real as it gets, NO CAMERA TRICKS. **We all know the time it takes to find entertainment for an Event like yours. Scheduling this show at this time will reduce cost by eliminating the time it would normally take for you to research and find entertainment for your Event. People will come up to you and congratulate you on a great event – EVEN IF YOU DON'T WANT THEM TO! People will talk about the event YOU hosted long after the night is over.**
- **CONVENTIONS** – This usually incorporates some stage and a lot of walk around / strolling illusions. This has shown to be a success among organizations that sponsor trade shows and conventions. **We all know the time it takes to find entertainment for an Event like yours. Scheduling this show at this time will eliminate the time it would normally take for you to research and find**

entertainment for your Event. **Also,** Since conventions and trade shows often go over several days this option **minimizes costs** for the host organization **by reducing travel costs, reducing production expenses, and reducing various talent costs.** Dan will perform in intimate settings (small groups), large gatherings, walk around, etc based on the requirements of the group and or specific function.

*****(Get an idea of what sort of performance they want and then charge accordingly. **State the cost and then be silent!** If the client agrees, then send them the contract via email, collect the 50% and place the event on the schedule once you HAVE THE MONEY IN HAND). ONLY IF THE PROSPECT CLAIMS TO HAVE AN ISSUE WITH THE COST SHOULD YOU EVER CONSIDER ANY NEGOTIATION. If cost is a factor for the client then find out what sort of performance they are looking for. If they want to cut the Stage COST, then we MUST cut the Stage SHOW. Example: Let's imagine the Client can't spend $3,000 for a Stage show but wants it. Offer 30 minutes of Stage and 30 minutes of Close Up / Strolling Illusions for $2,250. This is ½ the cost of both shows and saves the Client $750.

Remember, the answers to the Qualifying Questions above will help you to determine to a large degree the budget of the prospective client.

ALWAYS get a 50% deposit because the gig is not yours until you have that money in your hand. If any agency claims they will not send 50% because they want to make sure you show up, then don't work with them. For all you know, they could go out of business and they're the ones who don't show up.

If the prospective client says they already have entertainment then use the following pitch

YOU: How many times have you booked the same entertainment? Wouldn't you agree that it would be nice to have something scheduled that you have never seen before? This is no magic show. This is pure mentalism.

Get the commitment by having the prospective client send an email to info@cainillusions.com summarizing the conversation. After you receive the email, send the Performance Agreement and Rider. If you can get the 50% at this time, then go for it. If a 50% down payment is not received to secure the date of the Event, then I will not appear.

This is the Performance Agreement that I will send over to the client via email once the deal is made:

Performance Agreement – Page 1

Client Information:
Contact Person:
Title:
Organization:
Address (of organization):
Phone: **Email**:
Description of Presentation: Center Presentation. 50 – 60 minutes of mind-reading and psychological manipulation, complete with audience participation and humor. No one in the audience knows who will share the stage with him next. This allows for the audience, as a whole, to experience the show on a larger scale while allowing an individual to enjoy it on a more personal level. Examples: A guest thinks of a loved one and performer reveals it. Performer creates a connection where one person is touched and the other feels it.
Date of Presentation: / /
Time of Presentation:
Location of Presentation:

The client agrees to pay the following fees and expenses:
The fee for this presentation is: $
A non-refundable 50% deposit of $_____ is due by __/__/__ to secure the engagement date. However, should (enter your name) miss the engagement due to illness or emergency, client will be reimbursed the deposit in full.
The remaining balance of $_____ to be handed to (Your Name) on engagement day
(before the performance) unless payment in full has already been made prior.
Please make checks payable to: (Your Name) and mailed to:
(Your Name)
(Your Address)

Performance Agreement – Page 2

Travel Expenses:

Airfare, ground transportation to the event, and lodging must be provided. (Waived)

AV Requirements:

One clip-on microphone **and** one wireless handheld microphone
(with stand). (Your Name) reserves the right to have a camera person(s) take pictures
and/or record his performance. Client grants (Your Name) permission to use said photographs and recordings for promotional use in print and internet-based media.

Equipment and Supplies:

One table (4-6 feet long). One bottled water.

Recording:

Client grants permission to (Your Name) to have a camera person(s) take pictures and/or
record his performance if he chooses. Client grants permission to (Your Name) to use
said photographs and/or recording for (Your Name) promotional use in print and/or
internet-based media.

This agreement shall be construed and governed by the laws of the State of (Your State)

even if signed by a Client in a different state. Our signatures on this agreement indicate
full compliance with the requests and the promises above, and complete understanding
of the services to be provided.

_____

_____   _____
Client   Date

_____   _____
(Your Name   Date

Speaking & Listening

As an entertainer you must be your own salesperson. Most salespeople who are "people persons" are good at selling whatever they have to offer. If you are not a "people person" then you need to learn real quickly how to become one.

It's easy to talk with people that you have a rapport with. But with our industry you have to build rapport with people outside of your comfort zone. You can't afford to not interact with people that you do not have natural rapport with. All you have to do to gain rapport is stretch your behavior outside your comfort zone until you mirror your prospect. For instance, match speech patterns with people to gain rapport outside of your typical sports or humdrum conversation.

Getting gigs is easy and fun when you are the one in control and closing the deal. It can be frustrating though, when you're trying to get the gig but are unsure how.

Take some of the stress off of your shoulders by focusing on motivating your potential clients. Place the responsibility back to your potential client to solve their own situation and the pressure to land the gig will be obsolete. When you're on the phone cold-calling, or talking face-to-face to your potential client, imagine your prospect with the letters "WIFM" stamped across their forehead. Imagine that with everything you say, your potential client is asking, "What's In it For Me?"

As a general rule, people care about how they can benefit from any situation. Whether that be a way to gain an edge, solve a problem or make their business a better place. Consider your presentation and how it can benefit your prospect instead of trying to sell them features of yourself.

Always take notes when talking with prospects. Listen closely to what your prospect is saying. Answer questions with benefits. Speak clearly and slowly. Don't be in a hurry to end a call. Smile while speaking – they can tell. Don't allow anything they may say intimidate you, or upset you, or frustrate you. Stay focused!

Listen throughout the entire call. You should listen to everything and anything your prospect may be telling you (directly or indirectly). You should listen to the voice characteristics of volume, rate of speech, tone and pitch to determine the prospects' frame of mind.

Take notes because writing something is ten times more likely to make you remember and understand than simply listening to it. Your notes will serve as a reminder of where each conversation (assuming there is more than one) is to the next and continue relationship development.

Don't be in a hurry to talk. Let your prospect talk to you. Let him or her tell you why they should do business with you.

The majority of individuals who have experienced fear when selling over the phone usually do so because of the following:

- Lack of confidence in themselves and their ability to build rapport.
- Did not have a thorough understanding of their craft/art.
- Were not speaking or listening properly.
- Thought about possibly being turned down or rejected by the person on the other end of the phone call.
- Felt that the person on the other end of the phone call was more intelligent or better informed.
- Forgot about the determination to succeed.

You can overcome fear of cold calling when you follow these rules:

- Always understand your craft/art
- Always speak and listen properly to the person on the other end of the line.
- Always try to present your pitch professionally.
- Always maintain and demonstrate self-confidence over the phone. Smile!
- Never apologize for calling anyone.
- Never give up! Always strive to succeed!

When you make telephone calls you are judged by your voice alone. Your voice IS you. Only by your voice will your prospect decide whether you're even worth listening to. Everything hinges in those few seconds on how your prospect hears you. Poor pronunciation and lazy enunciation can ruin even the best presentation. Here are some guidelines that may help you use your voice more effectively on the phone:

- Voice modulation and verbal presentation will set the tone for the call. Sounding positive and enthusiastic is a must for a successful call.
- The tone of your voice reveals your attitude even more than the rate of speech and can influence your prospects acceptance of the call. A tone of annoyance, fatigue or indifference cannot be missed by your prospect.
- Pitch is another key factor. Your voice naturally rises when you are interested, seeking or inquiring or anticipating.
- Be positive! Smile when you talk on the phone. A smile in your voice indicates to a prospect that you are happy and willing to help him or her with their business.
- Speak in a conversational tone of voice with just the right volume. By doing so you reduce the possibility of tension developing between you and your prospect.

Speak clearly and distinctly. Pronounce carefully each syllable and word. Don't slur your words. You will inspire trust and confidence in a prospect when you give strength to every word you say.

Talking on the phone doesn't give you the advantage of the face-to-face contact with your prospect. You can't read his or her body language or nonverbal communications. All you have is their tone of voice, what they say and how they say it. Studies have shown that the communications activity breaks down into these proportions:

- 9% Writing
- 16% Reading
- 30% Talking
- 45% Listening

Being a good listener takes work so people avoid it whenever they can. It always presents questions that need answering, problems that need solving. Most people feel they could use the time preparing what they're going to say when the talker gets finished. Have you ever been guilty of faking attention to a speaker while your mind wandered all over the place? This happens when your prospect is boring or uninteresting. Distractions take their toll on all who are listening. This can be tuned with a little effort. For example, if you are placed on hold waiting for the decision-maker to come to the phone, don't let your mind wander. Instead, make good use of this time. Think about what you are going to say to the prospect. Think about your attention-getting and interest-creating statements. If you don't, you'll be unprepared when your prospect comes to the phone.

Emotions are a barrier to communication and comprehension. They can make you hostile to your prospect's point of view or can make you unduly enthusiastic about it. Emotions are difficult to control. But when you can anticipate what they will do, you can recognize your reactions and say to yourself, "Wait a minute, let me take a step back and look at the facts for what they are." Don't be too overly anxious to tell your prospect everything at once. Don't be in a hurry to pour out all your features. Remember, listen to what the prospect wants so you can respond with the benefits you can provide.

So here are the basic principles:

- Limit your own talking
- Think like the prospect → WIFM
- Take time to listen
- Pay attention and take notes
- Work at listening
- Don't argue mentally or verbally.
- Be patient

Companies spend a lot of money on market research trying to figure out what customers and prospects want.

However, you conduct the best, most accurate and immediate form of market research every time you pick up the phone. Asking questions and listening. By listening, you learn exactly what you need to do to help your prospect. Lock in on every word and thought the speaker expresses as if your income depended on it.

Because it does.

There are open-ended questions to assure understanding. Communication is difficult at times, so when you must know exactly what the prospect wants or objects to, you should ask questions to force clarification. These may take the form of a restatement of the main points as they are understood.

For example: "Let me see if I understand." Repeat what the prospect said, then ask, "Do I have the right idea?"

Do not—I repeat—Do not imply by the wording of your questions that the prospect has just done a poor job of explaining or doesn't have a good command of the language. That is what opening's like these would imply: "What you mean to say is…."

Don't make your prospect look inferior. People dislike being told anything. But they don't mind getting answers to questions.

You may run into a situation where your prospect is too busy and has no time to talk. This may be true or it may be just one more way of trying to "blow you off the phone." Whatever the case, try to do the following:

- Acknowledge the fact the your prospect is busy. Explain that most successful people are.
- Explain that you had a similar situation with another prospect and as soon as you explained what you could do for him, he made this time to listen.

If the prospect still insists he/she doesn't have the time to talk, don't push the issue. Explain that you have a service from which he/she will reap many benefits. Ask what time will be more convenient. Then make sure you call that prospect back.

If you are in the position to "hire" sales people to make calls for you then I offer the following contract you can utilize. You may change what you need to suit your situation:

INDEPENDENT CONTRACTOR AGREEMENT

This Independent Contractor Agreement (this "Agreement") is made effective as of (month) (day) , 2013, by and between (Your company and address), and (Client Name) , of (Client Address). In this Agreement, the party who is contracting to receive the services shall be referred to as the "Company", and the party who will be providing the services shall be referred to as "Client".

1. **DESCRIPTION OF SERVICES.** Beginning on (Month Day Year) Client will provide the following services (collectively, the "Services"): As an Independent Contractor, generate prospect leads of high-end businesses that generate no less than one million dollars ($1,000,000.00) in revenue per year. Actively pursuing those targeted prospects to secure performances for the Company at rates agreed upon with the Company. Assist in developing a sales plan for growing the Company's base of clients. Represent the Company with professionalism. Be responsible for expenses incurred in the performance of the obligations incurred pursuant to this agreement.

2. **PAYMENT FOR SERVICES.** The Company will pay compensation to Client for the Services. Payments will be made as follows:

The Company agrees to pay Client commission on performances secured. Performances will be recorded as secured when payment of 50% of agreed rate has been received by the Company. Client will receive 20% of the full rate which is to be paid from the initial payment received (50% of the agreed rate which is to secure the date of performance). Commission is not to be paid on any performance until at least 50% of the agreed rate has been received to secure the performance date. If repeat performances are secured as a result of Client closing the deal then commission on every repeat show of that account will be 12% of the agreed rate. A goal of $6,000.00 accumulative generated revenue per month will be set forth with no penalty if not met. However, if met, a BONUS of $300 will be paid to Client by the 15th of the following month. A second goal of $12,000.00 accumulative generated revenue per month will also be set forth with no penalty if not met. However, if met, a BONUS of $1,000.00 will be paid to Client by the 15th of the following month.

3. **TERM/TERMINATION.** This Agreement may be terminated by either party upon 14 days written notice to the other party.
4. **RELATIONSHIP OF PARTIES.** It is understood by the parties that Client is an independent contractor with respect to the Company, and not an employee of the Company. The Company will not provide fringe benefits, including health insurance benefits, paid vacation, or any other employee benefit, for the benefit of Client.
5. **WORK PRODUCT OWNERSHIP.** Any copyrightable works, ideas, discoveries, inventions, patents, products, or other information (collectively, the "Work Product") developed in whole or in part by Client in connection with the Services shall be the exclusive property of the Company. Upon request, Client shall sign all documents necessary to confirm or perfect the exclusive ownership of the Company to the Work Product.
6. **OWNERSHIP OF SOCIAL MEDIA CONTACTS.** Any social media contacts, including "followers" or "friends," that are acquired through accounts (including, but not limited to email addresses, blogs, Twitter, Faceboook, Youtube, or other social media networks) used or created on behalf of the Company are the property of the Company.
7. **CONFIDENTIALITY.** Client will not at any time or in any manner, either directly or indirectly, use for the personal benefit of Client, or divulge, disclose, or communicate in any manner any information and treat it as strictly confidential. This provision shall continue to be effective after the termination of this Agreement. Upon termination of the Agreement, Client will return to the

Company all records, notes, documentation and other items that were used, created, or controlled by Client during the term of this Agreement.

8. **INJURIES.** Client acknowledges Client's obligation to obtain appropriate insurance coverage for the benefit of Client (and Client's employees, if any). Client waives any rights to recovery from the Company for any injuries that Client (and/or Client's employees) may sustain while performing services under this Agreement and that are a result of the negligence of Client or Client's employees.

9. **INDEMNIFICATION.** Client agrees to indemnify and hold harmless the Company from all claims, losses, expenses, fees including attorney fees, costs, and judgments that may be asserted against the Company that result from the acts or omissions of Client, Client's employees, if any, and Client's agents.

10. **NON-COMPETE AGREEMENT.** For a period of one year after the termination of this Agreement, Client will not directly or indirectly engage in any business that competes with the Company. This covenant shall apply to the geographical area that includes (but may not be limited to) Delaware, New Jersey, Pennsylvania, Maryland, Virginia, New York, and Washington, D.C. Client agrees that this non-compete provision will not adversely affect the livelihood of Client.

11. **ENTIRE AGREEMENT.** This Agreement contains the entire agreement of the parties, and there are no other promises or conditions in any other agreement whether oral or written.

12. **SEVERABILITY.** If any provision of this Agreement shall be held to be invalid or unenforceable for any reason, the remaining provisions shall continue to be valid and enforceable. If a court finds that any provision of the Agreement is invalid or unenforceable, but that by limiting such provision it would become valid and enforceable, then such provision shall be deemed to be written, construed, and enforced as so limited.

13. **APPLICABLE LAW.** This Agreement shall be governed by the laws of the State of Delaware.

PARTY CONTRACTING SERVICES:

(Your Company)

By:

_____

    (Your Name)   Date
    Owner

CONTRACTOR:
(Client Name)

By:

_____

    (Client signature)   Date
    Independent Entertainment Contractor

Corporate Entertainer Dan Cain, Mentalist

Dan Cain, owner of Cain Illusions, LLC, is an experienced & seasoned corporate entertainer and close up illusion artist who guarantees success as after-dinner entertainment *or* an ice-breaker at trade shows for small or large corporate events. His demonstrations include experiments of that sixth sense, close up illusions, and comedic relief. He uses individuals in his audience who are unknown to him for his "telepathic" demonstrations and makes them the actual recipients of telepathy and mental pictures which he climactically reveals! Interest and thrills await those viewing this most entertaining presentation.

Dan is the only person in the history of Mentalism that *predicted,* with 100% accuracy, the winning team, final score, and a specific highlight of football's 46th Big Game in 2012 and donated all proceeds raised to the Children's Miracle Network John's Hopkins Children Center. You can see some of the media coverage here: http://www.cainillusions.com/Media.html

Dan Cain, WWW.CAINILLUSIONS.COM

www.ingramcontent.com/pod-product-compliance
Lightning Source LLC
Chambersburg PA
CBHW041150180526
45159CB00002BB/760